OHIO

The Buckeye State

BY
JOHN HAMILTON

Abdo & Daughters
An imprint of Abdo Publishing | abdopublishing.com

abdopublishing.com

Published by ABDO Publishing, a division of ABDO, PO Box 398166, Minneapolis, Minnesota 55439. Copyright © 2017 by Abdo Consulting Group, Inc. International copyrights reserved in all countries. No part of this book may be reproduced in any form without written permission from the publisher. ABDO & Daughters™ is a trademark and logo of ABDO Publishing.

Printed in the United States of America, North Mankato, Minnesota.
052016
092016

Editor: Sue Hamilton   **Contributing Editor:** Bridget O'Brien
Graphic Design: Sue Hamilton
Cover Art Direction: Candice Keimig   **Cover Photo Selection:** Neil Klinepier
Cover Photo: iStock
Interior Images: Alamy, AP, Carl Stokes Family, Cincinnati Bengals, Cincinnati Reds, Cleveland Browns, Cleveland Cavaliers, Cleveland Indians, Columbus Blue Jackets, Columbus Crew SC, Corbis, DenPro, Dreamstime, Geoff Mason, Getty, Glow Images, The Goodyear Tire & Rubber Company, Granger Collection, Gunter Kuchler, History in Full Color-Restoration/ Colorization, iStock, Library of Congress, Mile High Maps, Mountain High Maps, One Mile Up, NASA, Ohio Dept of Natural Resources, Ohio Historical Society, Ohio History Connection, Ohio State University, Skye Marthaler, Smithsonian, Thinkstock, TourismOhio, & Wikimedia.

Statistics: *State and City Populations*, U.S. Census Bureau, July 1, 2015/2014 estimates; *Land and Water Area*, U.S. Census Bureau, 2010 Census, MAF/TIGER database; *State Temperature Extremes*, NOAA National Climatic Data Center; *Climatology and Average Annual Precipitation*, NOAA National Climatic Data Center, 1980-2015 statewide averages; *State Highest and Lowest Points*, NOAA National Geodetic Survey.

Websites: To learn more about the United States, visit booklinks.abdopublishing.com. These links are routinely monitored and updated to provide the most current information available.

Cataloging-in-Publication Data

Names: Hamilton, John, 1959- author.
Title: Ohio / by John Hamilton.
Description: Minneapolis, MN : Abdo Publishing, [2017] | Series: The United
    States of America | Includes index.
Identifiers: LCCN 2015957734 | ISBN 9781680783377 (lib. bdg.) |
    ISBN 9781680774412 (ebook)
Subjects: LCSH: Ohio--Juvenile literature.
Classification: DDC 977.1--dc23
LC record available at http://lccn.loc.gov/2015957734

CONTENTS

THE BUCKEYE STATE

Ohio packs a big punch in a little package. It is one of the smallest states west of the Appalachian Mountains. Yet, its booming population has turned the state into a manufacturing powerhouse, and Ohio's many farms feed a hungry nation. Ohio isn't a big state, but it holds more than 11 million people, making it the 7th-most populous state in the country.

Ohio is nicknamed "The Buckeye State" because of its many buckeye trees. (The nuts of the tree resemble the eyes of a male deer.) During Ohio's early pioneer days, settlers cut down many of the trees to build log cabins.

Today, Ohio is rich with natural resources, including rivers and lakes for transportation, and good soil for farming. Thanks to its resources and its central location, Ohio's busy factories ship goods all over the nation and the world. In recent years, service industries such as health care and education have also become very important to Ohio.

Ohio's successful farms, together with the state's vast transportation system, help feed the world.

The Rock and Roll Hall of Fame and Museum in Cleveland, Ohio, receives thousands of visitors every year.

QUICK FACTS

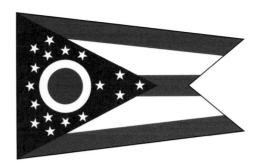

Name: Ohio is an Iroquois Native American word that means "great river." It refers to the present-day Ohio River.

State Capital: Columbus, population 835,957

Date of Statehood: March 1, 1803 (17th state)

Population: 11,613,423 (7th-most populous state)

Area (Total Land and Water): 44,826 square miles (116,099 sq km), 34th-largest state

Largest City: Columbus, population 835,957

Nickname: The Buckeye State

Motto: With God All Things Are Possible

State Bird: Cardinal

State Flower: Scarlet Carnation

State Gemstone: Flint

State Tree: Buckeye

State Song: "Beautiful Ohio"

Highest Point: Campbell Hill, 1,550 feet (472 m)

Lowest Point: Ohio River, 455 feet (139 m)

Average July High Temperature: 84°F (29°C)

Record High Temperature: 113°F (45°C), in Gallipolis on July 21, 1934

Average January Low Temperature: 20°F (-7°C)

Record Low Temperature: -39°F (-39°C), in Milligan on February 10, 1899

Average Annual Precipitation: 40 inches (102 cm)

Number of U.S. Senators: 2

Number of U.S. Representatives: 16

U.S. Presidents Born in Ohio: Ulysses Grant (1822-1885); Rutherford Hayes (1822-1893); James Garfield (1831-1881); Benjamin Harrison (1833-1901); William McKinley (1843-1901); William Taft (1857-1930); Warren Harding (1865-1923)

U.S. Postal Service Abbreviation: OH

QUICK FACTS

GEOGRAPHY

Ohio is in the north-central part of the United States. It is part of the Midwest region, which is also called the Heartland. It covers 44,826 square miles (116,099 sq km) of land and water, making it the 34th-largest state.

Ohio's highest point is Campbell Hill, in the west-central part of the state. It is 1,550 feet (472 m) high. The lowest point is just 455 feet (139 m) above sea level. It is in the southwest, where the Ohio River exits the state.

Ohio's neighbor to the north is Michigan. Pennsylvania is to the east. To the west is Indiana. The long, winding Ohio River forms the state's southern border with Kentucky and West Virginia. About two-thirds of Ohio's northern border is bound by Lake Erie, one of the Great Lakes.

Cincinnati, Ohio

Covington, Kentucky

Ohio River

The Ohio River forms the border between Ohio and Kentucky.

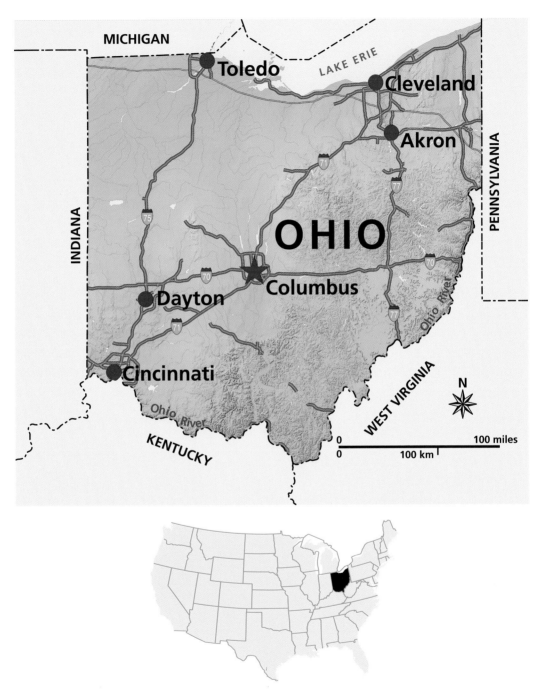

Ohio's total land and water area is 44,826 square miles (116,099 sq km). It is the 34th-largest state. The state capital is Columbus.

Most of Ohio's western half is part of a region called the Central Lowland. Formed by the power of ancient glaciers, it is mostly flat. There are also some gently rolling hills. The fertile soil is good for growing crops. A large part of the region is called the Till Plains, but there is also a narrow strip of lowlands next to Lake Erie that is called the Great Lakes Plains.

Thousands of years ago, Ice Age glaciers covered much of Ohio. These enormous sheets of ice were up to one-mile (1.6-km) thick. When the massively heavy glaciers crept across the land, they ground up the bedrock. After the ice sheets melted, about 10,000 to 14,000 years ago, they left behind clay, sand, gravel, and pebbles. Wind and water erosion, plus centuries of composted prairie grasses, created today's black soil that is perfect for growing crops.

Ohio's farmland is mostly flat, with some gently rolling hills.

A heavily wooded part of Ohio at Sprucevale Lookout, near Little Beaver Creek State Park, close to the border of Pennsylvania.

Glaciers did not reach into most of the eastern third of Ohio. Called the Appalachian Plateau, it is a region of steeply wooded ridges and deep valleys. The southeastern corner is especially rugged. The thin soil makes for poor farming. There are, however, large deposits of coal in the region.

Ohio gets its name from the Ohio River, which forms the state's southern border. The river flows to the southwest, eventually emptying into the Mississippi River far downstream. The Ohio River is the largest tributary, by water volume, of the Mississippi River. Other major rivers in Ohio include the Cuyahoga, Miami, Maumee, Muskingum, Scioto, and Sandusky Rivers.

CLIMATE AND
WEATHER

Ohio has a humid continental climate. Summers are hot and humid, while winters are cool and cloudy. Ohio's record high temperature occurred in the town of Gallipolis on July 21, 1934. That day, the thermometer soared to 113°F (45°C). The state's record low was -39°F (-39°C). It occurred in Milligan on February 10, 1899.

Cold air masses from Canada often sink over Ohio. Warm, tropical air from the Gulf of Mexico also travels over the state. These air masses sometimes collide, causing rain. Ohio receives 40 inches (102 cm) of average yearly precipitation.

Lightning flashes across the sky during a summer storm near Canton, Ohio.

A bicycle messenger deals with lake-effect snow in Cleveland, Ohio.

Severe weather, including tornadoes, sometimes strike the state, but not as often as in states farther to the west that are deeper into Tornado Alley. On average, Ohio is struck by 19 twisters each year.

Statewide, Ohio receives about 28 inches (71 cm) of snowfall yearly. However, areas in the north receive much more snow, as much as 68 inches (173 cm) yearly in Cleveland. As winter weather systems drift across Lake Erie, they pick up evaporated water. When the clouds blow over the land, they dump massive amounts of lake-effect snow.

CLIMATE AND WEATHER

PLANTS AND
ANIMALS

Before European settlers came to Ohio, huge hardwood forests covered the state. Most of the trees were cut down to create farmland and construct houses. Over the years, many of the forests have been replanted. Today, about 31 percent of Ohio's land area is woodland. That is about 8.1 million acres (3.3 million ha).

The most common tree species in Ohio include red maple, sugar maple, yellow poplar, black cherry, northern red oak, white oak, black oak, white ash, shagbark hickory, sycamore, American beech, aspen, cottonwood, and elm. The official state tree is the Ohio buckeye. When the trees bloom, they have clusters of yellow-colored flowers.

Buckeye nuts are said to resemble the eyes of a male deer (a buck). "Buckeye" has become a nickname for anyone from Ohio, but especially anyone who attends Ohio State University in Columbus, Ohio.

Buckeye

Buckeye Tree Flowers and Bee

Butterfly Weed and Monarch Caterpillar

Common prairie wildflowers in Ohio include butterfly weed, blazing star, and purple coneflower. Cardinal flowers and swamp rose mallow are found in wetlands. Woodland wildflowers, such as wild geranium and red trillium, add splashes of color to Ohio's forest floors.

Swamp Rose Mallow

Red Trillium

White-Tailed Deer

Ohio's official state animal is the white-tailed deer. The name comes from the white color on the underside of their tails, which they flash when running away. Adult male deer (bucks) can weigh up to 250 pounds (113 kg).

The only other large mammals in Ohio are black bears and bobcats, but they are rarely sighted. There are dozens of smaller mammals that are native to the state. They include foxes, coyotes, groundhogs, opossums, rabbits, beavers, and raccoons. Striped skunks can spray their musk with great accuracy up to 15 feet (5 m) away. Pygmy shrews are one of the smallest mammals on Earth. They weigh as little as 2 grams, about the same as a dime!

Pygmy Shrew

Cardinals

About 350 species of birds make their home in Ohio. Common birds include doves, bluebirds, starlings, herons, kingfishers, falcons, larks, mockingbirds, owls, and woodpeckers. Game birds include ducks, geese, pheasants, and turkeys.

By the late 1970s, there were only a few bald eagles left in Ohio. Insecticides, used to kill mosquitoes, poisoned and nearly killed all the bald eagles also. Today, there are several hundred eagles living in the state. They are found mainly in the marshy region near western Lake Erie.

The state bird of Ohio is the cardinal. Males have a bright-red coloring and a loud, whistling song. Cardinals are yearlong residents of Ohio.

Common fish found lurking in the lakes and rivers of Ohio include trout, walleye, muskellunge, perch, bullheads, catfish, and bass.

HISTORY

People lived in present-day Ohio as early as 15,000 years ago. These Paleo-Indians were the ancestors of today's Native Americans. They were nomads who hunted herds of mastodons and mammoths for food. They used crude tools such as stone spear points made of flint. They also fished and gathered plants.

People of the Woodland Culture first appeared about 3,000 years ago. Their culture lasted for hundreds of years. They lived in villages and grew crops such as corn and squash. They also built huge mounds of dirt. Many were shaped like bears, deer, birds, or other animals. The earthworks were used for religious ceremonies, such as burials. Many can still be seen in Ohio today.

People of the Woodland Culture built circular mounds of dirt for religious ceremonies.

People of the Mississippian Culture lived in villages and built stockades for protection.

About 1,000 years ago, people of the Mississippian Culture moved into Ohio. (The Ohio branch is sometimes called the Fort Ancient people.) They lived in large villages that were protected by stockades, and grew corn and other vegetables. Around 1650, these people were driven out of Ohio by powerful Iroquois Native Americans. The Iroquois came from the East. They wanted the area's beaver pelts to sell to Europeans. The pelts were prized for making hats. They could be traded for weapons and supplies.

French and British explorers came to the Ohio area in the late 1600s and early 1700s.

The Iroquois Native Americans mostly hunted in the Ohio area. A small number lived there permanently. By the time Europeans came to Ohio in the late 1600s, there were few people living there. Several Native American tribes settled the Ohio area later, in the mid-1700s. They included the Miami, Huron, Shawnee, Delaware, and Iroquois people.

In the late 1600s, French explorers became the first Europeans to see the Ohio area. They included René-Robert Cavelier, Sieur de La Salle and Louis Jolliet. France claimed the land. However, Great Britain also wanted to control the area. There were many riches that both countries wanted, especially furs.

In the mid-1700s, France and Great Britain, together with their Native American allies, fought battles over their North American territories. The French and Indian War lasted from 1754 to 1763. Great Britain won the war. France lost its lands east of the Mississippi River, including present-day Ohio.

In 1775, Great Britain went to war against its American colonies, which wanted independence. In 1783, Great Britain lost the American Revolution. Ohio changed hands again. It became part of the newly formed United States.

In the late 1780s, Ohio was part of the Northwest Territory. It included the present-day states of Ohio, Indiana, Illinois, Michigan, Wisconsin, and a part of Minnesota.

Settlers poured into the Ohio area. On March 1, 1803, Ohio became the 17th state in the Union. It was the first state to be carved from the Northwest Territory. It became a very important farming state. Many big cities were also built.

After the American Revolution ended, settlers poured into the Ohio area. It became an important farming state.

Many slaves escaped to freedom through Ohio's Underground Railroad.

In the years before the Civil War, thousands of African American slaves fled the South. Many used the Underground Railroad in Ohio. It was a network of paths and safe houses where slaves could be sheltered and led to freedom.

The bloody Civil War raged from 1861 to 1865. The country was divided over slavery. Ohio sent about 320,000 troops to fight on the side of the Union against the pro-slavery Southern Confederacy. Nearly 7,000 Ohio soldiers died fighting in the war. Ohio was the home state of three famous Union generals: Ulysses S. Grant, William T. Sherman, and Philip H. Sheridan. Grant was later elected president of the United States in 1868.

After the Civil War, many important industries developed in Ohio. The state was the home of Wilbur and Orville Wright. From their bicycle workshop in Dayton, Ohio, the brothers designed and built the first powered flying machine that could be steered. (The first successful flight of the *Wright Flyer* airplane took place in 1903 in North Carolina).

The Wrights with their second powered airplane at Huffman Prairie near Dayton, Ohio, in May 1904.

During the 20th century, Ohio met many challenges. The Great Depression started in 1929 and lasted nearly a decade. Many Ohioans lost their jobs. After World War II (1939-1945), the economy improved as industries such as steel, oil, chemicals, and rubber became leading employers. However, starting in the 1970s, many of Ohio's big industries suffered because of competition from foreign companies.

Orville Wright flies over the trees at Huffman Prairie in November 1904.

Today, Ohio's economy has diversified and improved. Electronics, banking, and bioscience companies have added many jobs. They join farming and manufacturing in giving Ohio one of the strongest economies in the country.

DID YOU KNOW?

Serpent Mound Sketch

Serpent Mound

• Serpent Mound was built by ancient cultures of Ohio, starting about 2,300 years ago. Shaped like a giant snake that twists and bends around the landscape, it is 3 feet (.9 m) high and 1,348 feet (411 m) long. That makes it the largest effigy (likeness) of a serpent in the world. It was probably used for religious ceremonies. Archaeologists continue to discover clues that reveal exactly who built the mound, and why. Located in Adams County in southern Ohio, Serpent Mound has been designated a National Historic Landmark. Visitors can walk around the site, and tour the nearby Serpent Mound Museum, which is run by the Ohio Historical Society.

• John Chapman planted apple nurseries and orchards in the early 1800s. He moved from place to place, but spent much time in Ohio. Known as "Johnny Appleseed," he introduced apple trees to many communities on the American frontier. He was a friendly person who wore plain clothes and often walked barefoot. He was also a vegetarian, and was kind to animals. Chapman planted thousands of apple trees in Ohio. Today, people can learn more about him at the Johnny Appleseed Educational Center & Museum at Urbana University in Urbana, Ohio.

• During the War of 1812 (1812-1815), the United States and Great Britain fought a major naval battle on Lake Erie. On September 10, 1813, nine U.S. Navy vessels squared off against six British warships near Put-in-Bay, off the Ohio coast. Led by Commodore Oliver Perry, the Navy won the battle against the British. Afterwards, Perry wrote to his superiors and said, "We have met the enemy, and they are ours." The victory assured the American control of Lake Erie, preventing British attacks on Ohio, Pennsylvania, and western New York.

DID YOU KNOW?

PEOPLE

LeBron James (1984-) is a National Basketball Association (NBA) superstar who plays for the Cleveland Cavaliers. Born in Akron, Ohio, he shot hoops for St. Vincent-St. Mary's High School in his hometown. During his freshman year, the team went 27-0. At age 18, James was the number-one pick in the 2003 draft to play forward for the Cleveland Cavaliers. In his first season, he averaged nearly 21 points per game, and was the youngest player to ever be named NBA Rookie of the Year. After several successful seasons, James joined the Miami Heat in 2010. The Heat won back-to-back NBA championships in 2012 and 2013. James returned to Cleveland in 2014 with much fanfare. In 2016, he helped lead the Cavaliers to victory in the NBA Finals.

Neil Armstrong (1930-2012) commanded the Apollo 11 NASA Moon mission, flying with fellow astronauts Buzz Aldrin and Michael Collins. On July 20, 1969, Armstrong descended to the Moon in the *Eagle* landing module, along with Aldrin. Armstrong expertly piloted the *Eagle* to a safe landing on the lunar surface. Shortly afterward, he became the first person to set foot on the Moon, saying, "That's one small step for a man. One giant leap for mankind." Armstrong was born in Wapakoneta, Ohio.

John Glenn (1921-) in 1962 became the first NASA astronaut to orbit the Earth in a spacecraft. He flew in the *Friendship 7* Project Mercury mission. He was one of the original Mercury Seven group of NASA astronauts. After his NASA career, he served as a United States senator for the state of Ohio from 1974 to 1999. In 1998, while still a senator, he became an astronaut again, flying on space shuttle *Discovery* and becoming the oldest person to fly in space, at age 77. Glenn was born in Cambridge, Ohio.

Annie Oakley (1860-1926) was a sharpshooter who could fire a gun and almost always hit the target. As a child, she learned to shoot while hunting in the Ohio woods for game for her poor family. She joined Buffalo Bill's Wild West show in 1885 as a featured performer. Oakley was one of America's first celebrity superstars. In 1894, she starred in Thomas Edison's Kinetoscope film *Little Sure Shot*. Oakley was born near Willowdell, Ohio.

Thomas Alva Edison (1847-1931) was one of the busiest inventors of all time. He held 1,093 U.S. patents. His work changed the way most people lived. Edison's inventions included long-lasting electric light bulbs, recorded music, and motion pictures. He conducted research to find a rubber plant that could be grown in the United States to use in the automobile tire industry, and he built an electric power station. Edison was born in Milan, Ohio.

Granville T. Woods (1856-1910) was another great Ohio inventor. He wasn't as famous as Thomas Edison, but his work was so important that he became known as "The Black Edison." He started out self-taught. Woods invented a steam furnace and egg incubator, but he was most famous for his railroad devices. They included an automatic brake and a telegraph that worked on a moving train. Woods was born in Columbus, Ohio.

Toni Morrison (1931-) is an author who uses poetic language to tell stories of African American life. Her books are praised for their use of historical details, interesting dialogue, and complex characters. Her best-known novels include *The Bluest Eye*, *Sula*, *Song of Solomon*, and *Beloved*. Morrison won the Pulitzer Prize for Fiction in 1988 for *Beloved*. In 1993, she won the Nobel Prize for Literature. Morrison was born in Lorain, Ohio.

CITIES

Columbus is the capital of Ohio. It is also the state's largest city. Located near the center of Ohio, its population is approximately 835,957. Together with its suburbs and surrounding communities, the entire Columbus metropolitan area is home to almost 2.4 million people. Founded in 1812, the city is named for Christopher Columbus. It began as a center for fur trading. Today, the city has a strong economy. Major employers include insurance, banking, aviation, education, health care, and advanced technology. There are also many government jobs, since Columbus is the state capital. Ohio State University is one of the biggest universities in the nation. It enrolls more than 58,000 students.

Cleveland is the second-largest city in Ohio. Its population is 389,521. It is located on the south shore of Lake Erie, in the northeastern corner of the state. Cleveland became a transportation center in the 1800s when canals and railroads connected the city to the nation. The city became a major manufacturing center and steel producer. Today, other important businesses include health care, biotechnology, and insurance. The largest private employer in the city is the Cleveland Clinic, the world-renowned hospital and research center. The Rock and Roll Hall of Fame and Museum, located along the Lake Erie waterfront, attracts hundreds of thousands of visitors to Cleveland each year.

Cincinnati is the third-largest city in Ohio. Its population is 298,165. It is located on the shores of the Ohio River in the southwestern part of the state. Many large companies make their home in Cincinnati. They include Macy's, Kroger, and Procter & Gamble, the maker of many household products such as Crest toothpaste and Ivory soap. The city is also home to the University of Cincinnati.

Toledo is Ohio's fourth-largest city. About 281,031 people make the city their home. It is located in northwestern Ohio, along the Maumee River, near the western tip of Lake Erie. It is a busy manufacturing and transportation center, with easy access to railroads and the Great Lakes. The city's factories are known for making glass, car parts, plastics, and many other goods. The University of Toledo enrolls more than 23,000 students.

Akron is located in northeastern Ohio, just south of Cleveland. Its population is 197,859, which makes it Ohio's fifth-largest city. Akron was once nicknamed "The Rubber Capital of the World" because so many tire manufacturers were in the city. Today, Akron remains the home of The Goodyear Tire & Rubber Company. The celebrated Akron Symphony Orchestra performs at E.J. Thomas Hall at the University of Akron.

Dayton is the sixth-largest city in Ohio. Its population is 141,003. It is located in the southwestern part of the state, between Cincinnati and Columbus. Dayton is the city where Orville and Wilbur Wright developed and constructed the world's first airplane in 1903. Today, the city is home to industries such as aerospace, engineering, insurance, health care, and transportation. The National Museum of the United States Air Force is at Wright-Patterson Air Force Base, just northeast of the city. It displays more than 360 historical aircraft and missiles.

TRANSPORTATION

R ivers and canals were the superhighways of the 1800s. In Ohio, a 1,000-mile (1,609-km) network of canals once connected Lake Erie in the north with the Ohio River to the south. Today, water transportation remains a chief method of transporting goods into and out of the state. There are major ports along the Ohio River and Lake Erie.

Ohio has 34 freight railroads hauling cargo on 5,288 miles (8,510 km) of track. The most common kinds of freight include coal, farm products, metal products, chemicals, scrap, stone, plus sand and gravel.

The Great Lakes cargo ship H. Lee White *unloads taconite (iron ore) in Cleveland, Ohio.*

Cleveland Hopkins International Airport is Ohio's busiest airport.

There are 123,297 miles (198,427 km) of public roadways in Ohio. Several interstate highways crisscross the state. Interstate I-70 runs east and west, passing through the capital of Columbus. Interstate I-71 runs northeast and southwest. It also passes through Columbus.

Ohio's busiest airports include Cleveland Hopkins International Airport, Port Columbus International Airport, and Dayton International Airport. Cleveland Hopkins International Airport is the state's busiest. In 2015, it handled more than 8.1 million passengers. One of the biggest United States Air Force bases in the country is Wright-Patterson Air Force Base. It is near the city of Dayton.

NATURAL
RESOURCES

Ohio's soil continues to be its most precious natural resource. Agriculture is one of the strongest industries in the state. There are about 74,400 farms in Ohio. Farmland covers roughly 14 million acres (5.7 million ha) of land. That is slightly more than half of Ohio's land area.

Most of Ohio's farmland is in the western half of the state. The total yearly market value of Ohio's agricultural products sold is about $10 billion. The most valuable crops include soybeans, corn, hay, wheat, tobacco, cabbage, strawberries, apples, and potatoes. Ohio's farmers also raise many hogs, sheep, chickens, turkeys, plus beef and dairy cattle.

Hay is harvested and baled on a farm in Somerset, Ohio. Farmland covers slightly more than half of Ohio's land area.

A coal mining operation near Salineville, Ohio.

There are many hardwood forests in Ohio's hilly eastern and southern regions. About 8.1 million acres (3.3 million ha) of Ohio is forestland. That is almost one-third of the state's land area. Timber is cut to make furniture, cabinets, flooring, doors, wooden pallets, and many other products. The most common trees harvested include red and white oak, maple, yellow poplar, hickory, and white ash.

Coal has been mined in eastern Ohio since 1800. There are large deposits in the eastern and southeastern parts of the state. Ohio also produces oil and natural gas. Other mining products include salt, limestone, dolomite, sandstone, plus sand and gravel.

NATURAL RESOURCES

INDUSTRY

Ohio has long been known for its factories and the many products they produce. Although manufacturing isn't as strong as it once was, it still represents about 17 percent of the state's economy.

Ohio's factories produce many goods. They lead the nation in making plastics, rubber, fabricated metals, electrical equipment, and many kinds of appliances. The state is also a big producer of steel and automobiles.

There are many scientific research, aerospace, and defense contracting companies in Ohio. They develop and make airplanes, missiles, space vehicles, and aircraft parts. Some companies partner with the state's many universities. NASA's Glenn Research Center is near Cleveland. It develops space and aeronautics technology. Aeronautical research is also conducted at Wright-Patterson Air Force Base near Dayton.

In recent years, the service industry has become a large part of Ohio's economy. Instead of making products, companies in the service industry sell services to other businesses and consumers. The industry includes businesses such as advertising, banking, financial services, health care, insurance, restaurants, retail stores, law, marketing, and tourism.

Tourism gives a major boost to Ohio. It adds about $40 billion dollars to the state's economy. Each year, Ohio hosts more than 200 million visitors. They spend enough money to support about 412,000 jobs.

The Goodyear Tire & Rubber Company's blimp, *Wingfoot One*, flies over the company's Akron, Ohio, headquarters.

SPORTS

O hio has many professional major league sports teams. The Cincinnati Bengals and the Cleveland Browns play in the National Football League (NFL). The Cincinnati Reds and the Cleveland Indians are Major League Baseball (MLB) teams. The Reds have won five World Series titles. The Indians have won twice.

The Cleveland Cavaliers play in the National Basketball Association (NBA). In 2016, the Cavaliers won their first NBA Finals championship. The Columbus Blue Jackets play in the National Hockey League (NHL). The Columbus Crew SC are a Major League Soccer (MLS) team. The Crew won the MLS Cup championship in 2008.

Brutus the Buckeye is the Ohio State mascot.

Ohioans love college sports, especially football. Ohio is home to eight college football teams that are highly ranked by the National Collegiate Athletic Association (NCAA). The Ohio State Buckeyes, from Columbus, have claimed seven national NCAA football championships. They won their first in 1942. In total, Ohio State has 18 men's and 19 women's teams in a wide variety of sports.

Fishing, boating, and hunting are very popular in Ohio, along with other outdoor sports. There are many lakes, rivers, and streams in the state. Ohio has 74 state parks and 21 state forests. Favorite activities include camping, hiking, biking, and rock climbing. In winter, Ohioans love cross-country skiing, ice fishing, snowmobiling, and iceboating.

ENTERTAINMENT

There are dozens of orchestras, theaters, dance troupes, and art museums in Ohio. The Cleveland Museum of Art is known all over the world for its collection of more than 45,000 works of fine art. Its Asian and Egyptian collections are especially famous. Founded in 1913, admission to the museum is free to the public. Hundreds of thousands of art lovers visit the museum each year.

The Rock and Roll Hall of Fame and Museum is located along the shores of Lake Erie in Cleveland. The museum features music and artifacts from the legends of rock, including Elvis, the Beatles, Pink Floyd, David Bowie, and many more. Since the museum opened in 1995, it has hosted more than 10 million visitors.

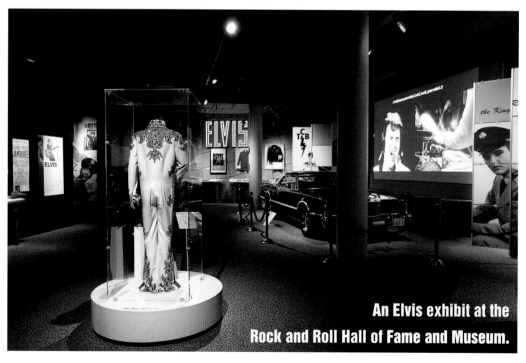

An Elvis exhibit at the Rock and Roll Hall of Fame and Museum.

Cedar Point Amusement Park is in Sandusky, Ohio. With 18 roller coasters, it is known as "The Roller Coaster Capital of the World."

The Pro Football Hall of Fame is in Canton, Ohio. It celebrates the careers of more than 300 football legends. In Akron, the National Inventors Hall of Fame highlights hundreds of men and women whose inventions have changed the world.

Ohio is known for its roller coasters. Cedar Point Amusement Park, in Sandusky, Ohio, is nicknamed "The Roller Coaster Capital of the World." It has 18 roller coasters, plus dozens of other thrill rides.

ENTERTAINMENT

TIMELINE

13,000 BC—The earliest Paleo-Indians arrive in the area of present-day Ohio. They lead a nomadic existence, hunting mammoths and bison.

1000 BC—People of the Woodland Culture appear in Ohio. They live in villages and grow crops.

1000—People of the Mississippian Culture move into the Ohio area. They grow corn and other crops.

1650—Iroquois Native Americans enter the Ohio area, hunting for beaver pelts. They drive out other Native American groups from the area.

Late 1600s—French explorers René-Robert Cavelier, Sieur de La Salle and Louis Jolliet enter the Ohio area.

1754-1763—Conflict over Ohio is one cause of the French and Indian War.

1783—The United States is awarded the Northwest Territories, including Ohio, from Great Britain.

1800—The first Ohio coal deposits are discovered.

1803—Ohio becomes the 17th state in the Union.

1832—The first canal between Lake Erie and the Ohio River opens.

1861—American Civil War begins. Ohio troops fight for the Union North.

1903—Ohio natives Orville and Wilbur Wright fly the world's first airplane.

1962—Ohioan John Glenn becomes the first American astronaut to orbit the Earth.

1963—The Pro Football Hall of Fame opens in Canton, Ohio.

1968—Carl Stokes becomes the mayor of Cleveland. He is the first African American elected mayor of a large American city.

1995—The Rock & Roll Hall of Fame and Museum opens in Cleveland, Ohio.

2008—A major blizzard strikes Ohio, closing roads and airports. Columbus receives a record-setting 20 inches (51 cm) of snow.

2014—The Ohio State University Buckeyes football team wins its seventh national championship.

2016—The Cleveland Cavaliers win the NBA Finals championship.

GLOSSARY

CANAL

A man-made river deep and wide enough for boat traffic. Canals are often shortcuts between cities or countries. People and cargo traveling on boats using canals can shorten their travel times.

GLACIER

When snow gathers near the poles or on mountains, it forms a slow-moving "river of ice" called a glacier. Ice Age glaciers thousands of years ago were sometimes more than one mile (1.6 km) thick. They carved and smoothed the land underneath them.

ICE AGE

An Ice Age occurs when Earth's climate causes a major growth of the polar ice caps, continental ice shelves, and glaciers. The ice sheets can be more than one mile (1.6 km) thick.

INSECTICIDES

Chemicals used to kill mosquitoes and other insects. The insecticide DDT was used in the United States from the 1940s until it was banned in 1972. DDT is poisonous to people and animals. The chemical nearly wiped out all the bald eagles in Ohio.

IROQUOIS

The Iroquois were a powerful Native American group. Member tribes included the Cayuga, Mohawk, Oneida, Onondaga, Seneca, and Tuscarora.

KINETOSCOPE

An early form of movie projector designed for one person at a time to view a film. It was invented by Thomas Edison and his employee William Dickson from 1888 to 1892. The name is a combination of Greek words: *kineto*, meaning "movement," and *scopos*, meaning "to view."

LAKE-EFFECT SNOW

A winter weather system that causes unusually large amounts of snow to fall. The weather systems pick up moisture when they blow over large bodies of water, such as Lake Erie, and then dump snow on land areas close to the shore.

NASA

A U.S. government agency started in 1958. NASA's goals include space exploration, as well as increasing people's understanding of Earth, the solar system, and the universe.

NOMADS

People who don't live in one place. Nomads travel constantly, hunting for food.

PATENT

A legal right, issued by a government, for an inventor to make, use, and sell a specific product.

TORNADO ALLEY

An area of the United States that has many tornadoes. There is no official boundary for Tornado Alley. Many maps show that it stretches from Texas in the south to North Dakota in the north. Some sources say it reaches east all the way to western Ohio.

TRIBUTARY

A river or stream that flows into a larger river. For example, the Ohio River flows into the Mississippi River. That makes the Ohio River a tributary of the Mississippi River.

INDEX